X-TREME FACTS: CONTINENTS

ASIA

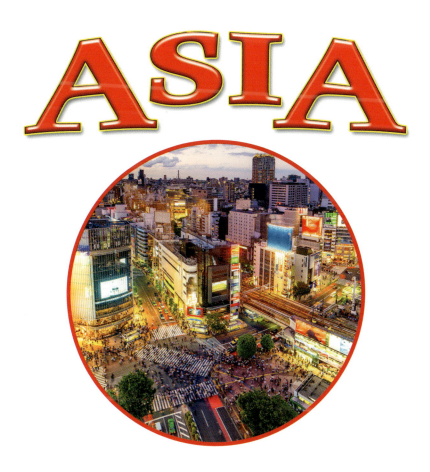

by Marcia Abramson

Minneapolis, Minnesota

Credits:

Title Page, 22 bottom, f11photo/Shutterstock; 4, Volina/Shutterstock; 5 top, Monkey Business Images/Shutterstock; 5 middle, dipsindia2004/Shutterstock; 5 bottom, AMINSEN/Shutterstock; 5 bottom left, 6 bottom right, 11 bottom left, 21 top left, 21 bottom left, LightField Studios/Shutterstock; 5 bottom middle, Alena Ozerova/Shutterstock; 5 bottom right, Nuttaya Maneekhott/Shutterstock; 6 top, travelwild/Shutterstock; 6 bottom, Lakeview Images/Shutterstock; 6 bottom left, Albert Kretschmer and Dr. Carl Rohrbach/Public Domain; 7 top right, Dimitrios Karamitros/Shutterstock; 7 top, Fanfo/Shutterstock; 7 top left, Dmitry Chulov/Shutterstock.com; 7 top middle, salajean/Shutterstock.com; 7 middle, SvetlanaSF/Shutterstock; 7 bottom, Guitar photographer/Shutterstock; 7 bottom left, Public Domain; 7 bottom right, From Album of the Yongzheng Emperor in Costumes/Public Domain; 8 top, Samrat Sengupta/Shutterstock; 8 bottom, AJP/Shutterstock.com; 8 bottom middle, Mihail Pustovit/Shutterstock; 8 bottom right,M ama Belle and the kids/Shutterstock; 9 top, Oppdowngalon/Shutterstock; 9 top middle, ANURAK PONGPATIMET/Shutterstock; 9 middle, MarinaDa/Shutterstock; 9 bottom, Alexandra Kovaleva/Shutterstock; 9 bottom left, Louella938/Shutterstock; 9 bottom right, Design Projects/ Di Studio/Shutterstock; 10 top, tscreationz/Shutterstock.com; 10 bottom, Katoosha/Shutterstock; 10 bottom middle, Golden Pixels LLC/Shutterstock; 11 top, sarin nana/Shutterstock; 11 top left, Thammanoon Khamchalee/Shutterstock; 11 top right, Jeka/Shutterstock; 11 middle left, Katvic/Shutterstock; 11 middle right, MasyuraN/Shutterstock; 11 bottom, Udompeter/Shutterstock; 11 bottom middle, altanaka/Shutterstock; 12 top, Alex Brylov/Shutterstock; 12, R.M. Nunes/Shutterstock; 13 top, Hung Chung Chih/Shutterstock.com; 13 top left,fi zkes/Shutterstock; 13 middle, Peyker/Shutterstock; 13 bottom, muzato/Shutterstock; 14 top, Averon/Shutterstock; 14 bottom, kaikups/Shuttèrstock; 14 bottom left, gianni31 joker/Shutterstock; 14 bottom right, Eleanor Scriven/Shutterstock.com; 15 top, sbellott/Shutterstock.com; 15 top left,A leksandar Todorovic/Shutterstock.com; 15 top center left, Massimo Vernicesole/Shutterstock.com; 15 top center right, Riyas kp/Shutterstock.com; 15 top right, angela Meier/Shutterstock; 15 bottom, Nepenthes/Creative Commons; 15 bottom left, barbaliss/Shutterstock; 15 bottom middle, Indian concepts/Shutterstock; 15 bottom right,fi zkes/Shutterstock; 16 top, J.M.Lerma/Shutterstock; 16 middle, Lê Minh Phát/Creative Commons; 16 bottom, Rod Waddington/Creative Commons; 17 top, badahos/Shutterstock; 17 top left, Prostock-studio/Shutterstock; 17 middle, soft_light/Shutterstock; 17 bottom,P hotoSunnyDays/Shutterstock; 17 bottom left, Lucy.Brown/Shutterstock; 17 bottom right, GUNAWAN SIDIK/Shutterstock; 18 top, Sergey Uryadnikov/Shutterstock; 18 top left, Najma khatun/Shutterstock; 18 bottom, Conservationist/Shutterstock; 19 top right, Juhku/Shutterstock; 19 top left, Sergey Bogdanov/Shutterstock; 19 middle, Vladimir Turkenich/Shutterstock; 19 bottom, tristan tan/Shutterstock;19 bottom middle, Adones Bentulan/Shutterstock; 20 top left, GrooveZ/Shutterstock; 20 top right, Flowersofsunny/Dreamstime.com 20 bottom,t rabantos/Shutterstock; 20 bottom left, Roman Samborskyi/Shutterstock; 20 bottom right, Kuznetsov Dmitriy/Shutterstock; 21 top, Iuliia Shcherbakova/Shutterstock; 21 top right, William Moss/Shutterstock; 21 middle left, TTstudio/Shutterstock; 21 middle right, PredragLasica/Shutterstock; 21 bottom, Elmer nev valenzuela/Creative Commons; 22 top, ssguy/Shutterstock; 23 top, Mamunur Rashid/Shutterstock.com; 23 top left, Brocreative/Shutterstock; 23 top middle, Wirestock Creators/Shutterstock.com; 23 middle, ESB Professional/Shutterstock; 23 bottom, JeKLi/Shutterstock; 24 top, smspsy/Shutterstock; 24 bottom, Mikhail Varushichev/Shutterstock.com; 24 bottom left, margouillat photo/Shutterstock; 25 top, Prostock-studio/Shutterstock; 25 top left, Karl Allgaeuer/Shutterstock; 25 top middle, Esin Deniz/Shutterstock; 25 middle, stockcreations/Shutterstock; 25 bottom,D GLimages/Shutterstock; 26 top, maloff/Shutterstock; 26 middle, Rasto SK/Shutterstock; 26 bottom, Kristin F. Ruhs/Shutterstock; 26 bottom right, Azim Khan Ronnie/Creative Commons; 27 high top, Dudarev Mikhail/Shutterstock; 27 top, feiyuezhangjie/Shutterstock; 27 top left, Olena Yakobchuk/Shutterstock; 27 top right, Shang Xi/Public Domain; 27 middle, Olena Tur/Shutterstock; 27 bottom, Thavorn Rueang/Shutterstock.com; 27 bottom right, Sergey Novikov/Shutterstock; 28 top left, Gunarta/Creative Commons; 28 bottom left, Fpangestuphotographer/Creative Commons; 28 top right, PENpics Studio/Shutterstock; 28 bottom right, Yana Dziubiankova/Shutterstock; 29, Austen Photography

Bearport Publishing Company Product Development Team
President: Jen Jenson; Director of Product Development: Spencer Brinker; Managing Editor: Allison Juda; Associate Editor: Naomi Reich; Associate Editor: Tiana Tran; Art Director: Colin O'Dea; Designer: Elena Klinkner; Designer: Kayla Eggert; Product Development Assistant: Owen Hamlin

Produced for Bearport Publishing by BlueAppleWorks Inc.
Managing Editor for BlueAppleWorks: Melissa McClellan; Art Director: T.J. Choleva; Photo Research: Jane Reid

STATEMENT ON USAGE OF GENERATIVE ARTIFICIAL INTELLIGENCE
Bearport Publishing remains committed to publishing high-quality nonfiction books. Therefore, we restrict the use of generative AI to ensure accuracy of all text and visual components pertaining to a book's subject. See BearportPublishing.com for details.

Library of Congress Cataloging-in-Publication Data

Names: Abramson, Marcia, 1949- author.
Title: Asia / by Marcia Abramson.
Description: Minneapolis, Minnesota : Bearport Publishing Company, 2024. | Series: X-treme facts: continents | Includes bibliographical references and index.
Identifiers: LCCN 2023038307 (print) | LCCN 2023038308 (ebook) | ISBN 9798889164319 (library binding) | ISBN 9798889164395 (paperback) | ISBN 9798889164463 (ebook)
Subjects: LCSH: Asia--Juvenile literature.
Classification: LCC DS5 .A 27 2024 (print) | LCC DS5 (ebook) | DDC 950--dc23/eng/20230818
LC record available at https://lccn.loc.gov/2023038307
LC ebook record available at https://lccn.loc.gov/2023038308

Copyright © 2024 Bearport Publishing Company. All rights reserved. No part of this publication may be reproduced in whole or in part, stored in any retrieval system, or transmitted in any form or by any means, electronic, mechanical, photocopying, recording, or otherwise, without written permission from the publisher.

For more information, write to Bearport Publishing, 5357 Penn Avenue South, Minneapolis, MN 55419.

Contents

Awesome Asia! 4
A Long History 6
Climate Extremes 8
Long Rivers and Big Lakes! 10
Massive Mountains 12
Vast Deserts 14
Wonderful Asia 16
Amazing Animals 18
Island Nations 20
Sprawling Cities 22
Amazing Food 24
Extreme Fun 26

Make Paper Batik 28
Glossary 30
Read More 31
Learn More Online 31
Index 32
About the Author 32

Awesome Asia!

Earth's largest **continent** stretches from Israel to Japan and from Russia to Indonesia. Welcome to Asia! With so much land, it's not surprising that 60 percent of the world's population calls Asia home. What does it have to offer? It has both the highest and lowest points on Earth's surface. This awesome continent boasts some incredible animals, amazing cultures, and spectacular cities.

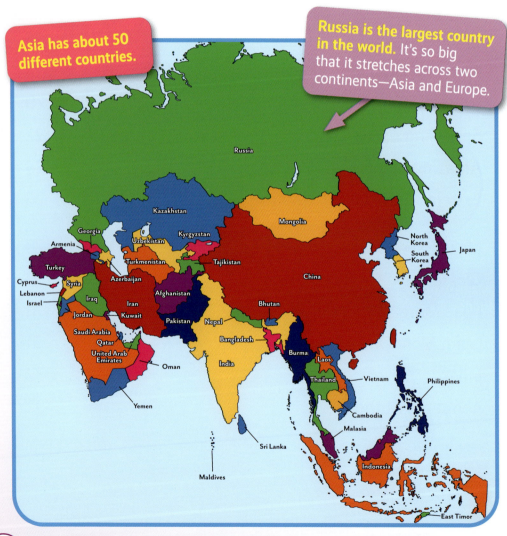

Asia has about 50 different countries.

Russia is the largest country in the world. It's so big that it stretches across two continents—Asia and Europe.

Asia takes up about 30 percent of Earth's land area.

Chinese is the most common language spoken in Asia. There are about 10 main varieties of this language, the most popular of which are Mandarin and Cantonese.

Sanskrit is one of Asia's oldest languages. Many languages have words borrowed from Sanskrit.

Asia is the birthplace of the world's major religions, including Buddhism, Christianity, Hinduism, Islam, and Judaism.

Yoga is a popular exercise all over the world. It originated thousands of years ago in Asia.

A Long History

Early humans first made their way into Asia more than 50,000 years ago. But it wasn't until about 12,000 years ago that they began to settle in one place. Soon, great **civilizations** arose throughout Asian river valleys, where the soil was ideal for farming. Mesopotamia dominated the land along the Tigris and Euphrates about 5,000 years ago. In the Indus River Valley, cities formed around what is present-day India, Pakistan, and Afghanistan. And the rich culture of **ancient** China started along the Yellow River and still continues today.

Petra, Jordan, was carved into sandstone cliffs more than 2,000 years ago.

YOU'RE LATE!

WELL, WHO ASKED YOU TO INVENT TIME!?

Mesopotamians came up with the 60-minute hour to keep time. They also created writing, math, and the wheel.

The Silk Road was a trade route that once stretched from Rome to China. A part has been paved over and is still in use today.

The earliest form of chess was played about 1,500 years ago in India.

Fireworks were invented in China sometime between 600 and 900 CE.

Climate Extremes

Be sure to pack lots of different clothes if you plan to visit Asia! Siberia in northern Russia has long, harsh winters, so bring a parka. You'll need it again for the snow-capped Himalayas. If you travel southwest, the climate warms up. Switch into shorts for the hot, dry Middle East. On the continent's eastern side, Japan, Korea, and much of China have changing seasons. And for Southeast Asia, you'll need a raincoat. It's warm and wet there.

Mawsynram, India, is the world's wettest place. Almost 40 feet (12 m) of rain falls there each year.

Monsoons whip up huge storms in south and east Asia.

The summer monsoon season brings heavy rainfall from April until September.

Asia also boasts the snowiest place on Earth—Japan.

Sapporo, Japan, has heated roads and sidewalks to help melt some of the 20 ft (6 m) of snow the city gets each year.

Aden, Yemen, is the driest place in Asia. It gets less than 2 inches (5 cm) of rain each year.

Oymyakon, Russia, gets colder than Mars! The record low is a bone-chilling -90 degrees Fahrenheit (-68 degrees Celsius).

Long Rivers and Big Lakes!

There are amazing bodies of water all across the continent. Asia's longest river, the Yangtze, winds through China's heartland for more than 3,900 miles (6,300 km). All along the river, there are huge farms and big cities. Boats of all sizes carry passengers and trade goods up and down the water. It's the same along the Mekong River in Southeast Asia. The continent is also home to some of the largest, deepest, and oldest lakes in the world!

The Ganges River in India provides fresh water to millions of people living nearby. It is also **sacred** to the Hindu people of the region.

LET'S GO DOWN AND CLEAN UP IN THE RIVER.

UHMM . . . I DON'T THINK THAT WATER WILL HELP.

China's Yellow River is the second longest in Asia. It's named for the yellowish mud that gives it its color.

The cleanest and clearest waters in Asia can be found at Kayangan Lake in the Philippines.

Massive Mountains

Many tall mountains tower over Asia. In fact, ten of the world's tallest mountains are in the Himalayas, running along the border of India and Tibet. The tallest peak is Mount Everest, which reaches about 29,000 ft (8,800 m) in the air. The Karakoram Mountains rise above parts of India, Pakistan, and China. And that's not the end of Asia's mountain mania!

> The Sherpa people have lived in the Himalayas for centuries. Many of their **traditional** songs and dances are about the magnificent mountains.

Long-haired mountain cattle called yaks help carry heavy loads up the Himalayas.

There are hundreds of Buddhist temples all across Tibet. Many of them are built high in the mountains.

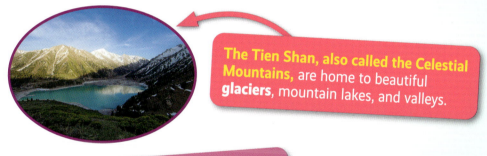

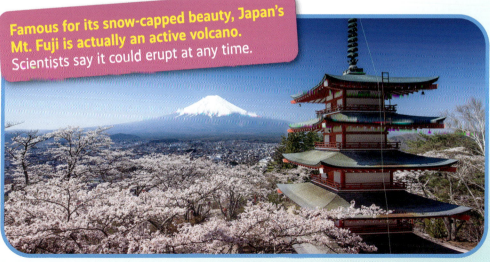

Mt. Fuji is considered sacred to many people in Japan. Temples can be found all over the volcano.

Vast Deserts

Asia has its fair share of deserts. For a sandy desert with blazing heat, head southwest to the Arabian **Peninsula**. The huge Arabian Desert is known for light-colored sand and temps as high as 130°F (55°C). Then there's the Gobi Desert in central Asia. It's a cold desert that's mostly rocky and sometimes even snowy. The Gobi lies north of the Himalaya Mountains, which block rain systems from getting through.

The Mogao Caves in the Gobi are a series of ancient Buddhist temples. Some date back to 366 CE.

The saxaul is one of the few kinds of tree that can grow in the Gobi. **It survives by storing water in its bark.**

People in the Gobi squeeze drinking water from saxaul bark and make a beautiful green dye from its wood.

The Bedouins are **nomadic** people of the Arabian Desert. **Some still live traditionally, herding animals and riding camels.**

The Arabian Desert covers about 900,000 square miles (2.3 million sq km), making it the fourth-largest desert in the world.

Rub' al-Khali is a giant stretch of sand in the southern Arabian Desert. The name means the empty quarter. **It's the largest area of sand in the world.**

Some of the sand **dunes** in Rub' al-Khali are more than 800 ft (250 m) high.

Wonderful Asia

With so many different landscapes and climates, it's no surprise that many different natural wonders can be found in Asia. Glaciers cover many mountain ranges across the continent, including more than 7,000 in Pakistan alone. Where mountains meet rushing rivers, you can see hundreds of amazing waterfalls. And the coast is dotted with sandy beaches that come in shades of gold, black, white, and even hot pink!

Hot lava carved hundreds of cave-like lava tubes on Jeju Island in South Korea. The volcanic island is a protected World Heritage Site.

Ban Gioc sits on the border between China and Vietnam. It is Asia's biggest water fall and is often called its most beautiful, too.

16

The Dead Sea in the Middle East is the lowest point on Earth's surface. Though it's named a sea, it's actually a very salty lake.

Almost nothing can live in the Dead Sea. But the salt does have its perks. It keeps people afloat at the water's surface.

The Chocolate Hills of the Philippines get their name from the chocolate-brown color of their grass in the summer.

Komodo Island in Indonesia is home to both pink beaches and the world's biggest lizard, the Komodo dragon.

17

Amazing Animals

Millions of years ago, dinosaurs roamed throughout Asia. Scientists are still discovering new dino **fossils** on the continent all the time. Today, Asia is still full of incredible critters. Giant pandas are considered a national treasure in China. King cobras slither through swamps in south and Southeast Asia. Orangutans live in the rain forests of Borneo and Sumatra, while tigers can be found across the continent. Let's take a closer look at Asia's amazing animals!

King cobras are the largest of all **venomous** snakes. **They have been known to grow up to 18 ft (5 m) long!**

The Komodo dragon of Indonesia can reach the size of a small car.

GET OUT OF MY WAY OR I'LL BITE YOU!

NOT IF I BITE YOU FIRST!

Komodo dragons are one of few species of lizard with a venomous bite.

The slow lorises of Southeast Asia are adorable with their fuzzy bodies and big eyes. **But watch out—they also have a venomous bite!**

Despite their name, red pandas aren't closely related to giant pandas. Instead, these mountain dwellers are distant cousins of raccoons and skunks.

Tigers are the world's biggest cats. Sorry, lions!

Beautiful snow leopards live in mountains across 12 countries, including Russia, China, India, and Pakistan.

Orangutans make tools from sticks to dig the seeds out of hard-shelled fruits.

Island Nations

A country that is surrounded by water or that is part of a bigger island is called an island nation. Asia has 10 of these unique places. Some, such as the Philippines and Japan, are spread across thousands of islands. Others, such as Singapore, have one main island and a few smaller ones. And the tiny nation of Brunei shares the island of Borneo with Indonesia and Malaysia. Together, island nations make up one-fifth of Asia.

More than a million cherry trees bloom every spring in Japan. Festivals are held all over the country to celebrate them.

Asia's smallest country is the Maldives. It has only about 115 sq miles (300 sq km) of land.

WHAT A BIG CITY! THERE MUST BE THOUSANDS OF PEOPLE LIVING THERE!

THIS DESERT ISLAND IS NOT THAT DESERTED AFTER ALL, IS IT?

Bahrain is a desert nation as well as an island nation. It's more than 90 percent desert.

20

Indonesia is the world's largest island nation. It is made up of about 17,500 islands.

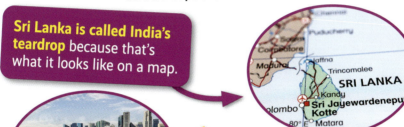

Sri Lanka is called India's teardrop because that's what it looks like on a map.

The city of Singapore is also the whole country of Singapore. **It's one of only three city-states in the world.**

There are more than 700 volcanoes in the Philippines. The island of Camiguin has seven volcanoes but only five towns!

Sprawling Cities

Almost half of Asia's people live in cities, and more are moving there every day. The world's three biggest cities are all in Asia. Tokyo, Japan, has 37 million people—the most in the world. New Delhi, India, comes in second with 32 million, but it's growing fast. Shanghai, China, is in third place with 29 million people living there. Let's visit some of these amazing places!

More movies are made in Mumbai, India, than in Hollywood, California. **Mumbai's movie business is called Bollywood!**

Shanghai has the world's longest transit system. It's more than 500 miles (830 km) long and is still growing.

WHY ARE YOU WEARING SUNGLASES AT NIGHT?

ALL THESE LIGHTS ARE SO BRIGHT!

Tokyo is famous for its **neon** signs and flashing lights.

More than a million tricycle-powered taxis called rickshaws ride through the streets of Dhaka, Bangladesh.

Korean pop music, also called K-pop, started in Seoul, South Korea. Now, it's popular around the world.

Beijing has been China's center of government for 800 years.

The city of Jerusalem in Israel is considered one of the oldest cities in the world. It's believed to be about 5,000 years old.

Amazing Food

Do you like ramen noodles? How about sushi or shish kebab? You can find all these foods and more in Asia. Every part of the continent has delicious food traditions that have spread worldwide. Many of the dishes include rice. More than 90 percent of the world's rice is grown and eaten in Asia. But in central Asia, Siberia, and the Middle East, wheat is a more common ingredient. It's often baked into pocket breads.

Japan made sushi popular worldwide, but it was first eaten in China.

Ice cream was a treat in China more than a thousand years ago.

Street vendors sell falafel all around the Middle East. The fried balls are made from beans or chickpeas.

Dolma means stuffed thing in Turkish. Dolmas are grape leaves stuffed with rice, meat, or other delicious fillings.

Spices help **preserve** food in India's hot climates. Curry powder is just one of the many different kinds you'll taste there.

In 2005, scientists found a 4,000-year-old bowl of noodles in China!

Extreme Fun

There are many ways to pass your days in Asia. China welcomes the Lunar New Year with a 15-day festival! People celebrate with fireworks, dances, and colorful lanterns. And festivals keep coming throughout the rest of the year across Asia. For a bit of history, you could visit Asia's many landmarks, such as Angkor Wat in Cambodia. Almost a thousand years ago, it was a city of temples. It's still considered the largest religious **monument** in the world. There's so much to enjoy about this extremely cool continent!

A giant gate in the shape of a lion guards the 1,500-year-old rock **fortress** of Sigiriya in Sri Lanka.

The world's tallest building, Burj Khalifa, towers over the city of Dubai in the United Arab Emirates.

THIS IS THE TIME TO SHOW SHOW ALL YOUR COLORS.

In India, people toss colored powder and water balloons at one another for Holi, the Festival of Colors.

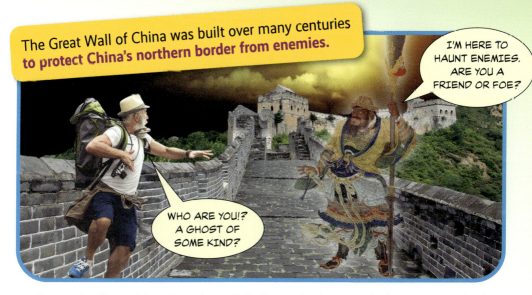

Some believe the Great Wall is haunted! People have reported seeing ghosts and hearing the sound of marching feet.

The Taj Mahal in India is often called the most beautiful building in the world.

The people of Thailand celebrate the new year in April with a national water fight called Songkran. People spray each other to chase away bad luck!

Make Paper Batik

Craft Project

Indonesian Batik is one of the many amazing artforms in Asia. Batik artists create these colorful pieces of art by using melted wax to draw patterns on cotton or silk fabric. When the fabric is dyed, the waxed parts don't pick up color, leaving behind beautiful designs. Make your own batik look on paper.

What You Will Need

- A piece of paper
- Crayons
- A small paintbrush
- A cup of water
- Watercolor paints
- Paper towel

Each batik pattern has a special meaning. A pattern called Mega Mendug is a reminder to be calm!

It can take a whole year to make a batik with lots of colors.

Step One

Draw a simple picture on your paper using crayons. Color it in with lots of bright colors.

Step Two

Crumple your paper into a little ball. Uncrumple it and crumple it again.

Step Three

Uncrumple your paper and smooth it out.

Step Four

Dip your brush in the water and then in the watercolor paint. Paint over the whole picture. If the brush gets dry, load it up with watery paint and continue. Use a paper towel to gently blot away excess paint. Leave it to dry.

ancient from a very long time ago

civilizations large groups of people who share the same history and ways of life

continent one of the world's seven large land masses

dunes large mounds of sand in a desert

fortress a building or group of buildings designed so they can be easily defended

fossils remains of plants or animals that lived long ago that have turned to stone

glaciers large masses of ice formed from firmly packed snow

monsoons strong storms that often bring heavy rain

monument a structure built to honor a person or event

neon a gas that lights up when electricity goes through it

nomadic roaming or wandering from place to place

peninsula a piece of land that sticks out into a body of water that almost completely surrounds it

plateau an area of high, flat land

preserve to keep something safe and stop it from changing

sacred very important or holy

species groups that living things are divided into according to similar characteristics

traditional relating to something that a group of people has done for many years

venomous full of poison that can be injected by a sting or bite

Read More

Aspen-Baxter, Linda. *Asia (Exploring Continents).* New York: Lightbox Learning Inc., 2023.

Finan, Catherine C. *Ancient China (X-treme Facts: Ancient History).* Minneapolis: Bearport Publishing Company, 2022.

Vonder Brink, Tracy. *Asia (Seven Continents of the World).* New York: Crabtree Publishing Company, 2023.

Learn More Online

1. Go to **www.factsurfer.com** or scan the QR code below.

2. Enter **"X-treme Asia"** into the search box.

3. Click on the cover of this book to see a list of websites.

Index

Arabian Desert 14–15
Bedouin 15
Dead Sea 17
dinosaurs 18
festivals 20, 26
food 24–25
glaciers 13, 16
Gobi Desert 14
Great Wall of China 27
Himalayas 8, 12, 14
islands 16–17, 20–21

lava 16
Mesopotamia 6
monsoons 8
mountains 8, 12–14, 16, 19
movies 22
population 4
rivers 6, 10–11, 16
Sanskrit 5
Sherpa 12
temples 13–14, 26
volcanoes 13, 21

About the Author

Marcia Abramson lives and works in Ann Arbor, Michigan, a sister city of Hikone, Japan.